TALES OF THE LOST POET

BY- AANSH IKA

TABLE OF CONTENTS

content:

<u>ACKNOWLEDGEMENT</u>

I extend my heartfelt gratitude and appreciation to everyone who has contributed to the creation and publication of this poetry collection, especially Canva; the manuscript was compiled and finalized by me on Canva and so I also extend the illustration copyrights to them.

To my family, whose unwavering support and understanding have been the bedrock of my creativity, thank you for inspiring me to explore the depths of emotion and experience.

To my friends, whose encouragement and enthusiasm have kept my passion for poetry burning bright, I am deeply grateful for your continuous belief in my work.

I am indebted to the poetry community, whose invaluable feedback and constructive criticism have helped refine and shape these verses into their final form.

My sincere thanks go to the team at the publishing house for their dedication, professionalism, and commitment to bringing this collection to life.

Last but not least, to the readers and lovers of poetry, thank you for embracing my words and allowing them to find a place in your hearts and minds.

With profound appreciation and warm regards,

Aansh Ika

Dedicated to the lost and seekers of the journey

EMBRACING SOULS OF DEBUT

In the dawn's soft glow, a dream unfurls,

Ink-stained fingers, crafting lyrical pearls.

Pages, a canvas for the soul's embrace,

A first poetry book, a sacred space.

In the quiet hum of the printing press,

Words birthed from the heart find their caress.

Eager verses, now bound in tender embrace,

A symphony of emotions, interlaced.

Each stanza a journey, a whispered plea,

In the boundless expanse of poetry's decree.

With trembling hope, and a bated breath,

The author unveils the soul's rich depth.

On shelves, it rests, a testament to time,

Echoing tales of life's rhythm and rhyme.

In the quiet corners where book lovers dwell,

A journey begins, the heart's secrets to tell.

In the eyes of readers, the words take flight,

Their spirits alight with each line's insight.

The author's voice, a celestial spark,

Igniting the souls adrift in the dark.

For within those pages, a world is spun,

A universe of feeling beneath the sun.

A first poetry book, a beacon of light,

Guiding lost souls through the darkest night.

With humble pride, and a grateful nod,

The poet whispers thanks to the universe, awed.

For the journey's beginning, a poetic art,

A first poetry book, a beating heart.

<u>EMBERS OF SORROW</u>

In the depths of shadows, where thelight retreats,

There walks a Witcher, in woes, he meets.

His heart, a cavern, where darkness thrives,

Forced to wield a silver blade, his soul connives.

Through the fog-draped woods, his steps resound,

A solitary figure, in sorrow bound.

Eyes like ember, smoldering in despair,

Haunted by the echoes of lives laid bare.

In the shimmering moon's forlorn embrace,

He grapples with demons, not of this space.

His touch, a bane, in a world so grim,

Where the line blurs 'tween righteous and sin.

His silver sword sings, with a mournful strain,

Cutting through hatred, yet bearing the stain.

For each life taken, a piece of him dies,

In the fading echoes of desperate cries.

A relic of destiny, carved in stone,

But the weight of his burdens, he bears alone.

A mask of indifference, shrouding the pain,

As he battles the darkness, for mankind's gain.

Yet, in the quiet moments, when the moon takes
flight,

He grapples with shadows, in the solace of night.

His heart, an abyss, where despair does roam,

A Witcher's life, a solitary tome.

WHISPERS OF DECEPTION AND ECHOES OF DESPAIR

Has the world deceived you?

Or have you ever deceived the world?

They say, world is valance, then,

Why lay on the ground curled?

You could be the elven king,

Or be a scared dwarf ,

And still be valued akin a thing;

Forever lost in realms, the old tales bring.

In the ancient groove where the spirits weep,

The restless ghosts their vigil keep.

Their mournful cry an ancient song,

Reverberating through the dusk so long.

Deep in the enchanted forest of the mind,

Where echoes of what could be, lay entwined.

The essence of potential takes it's form;

Amidst the tempest, it weathers the storm.

Oh, the threatening sadness that never sleeps,

Where tears of the night forever seep.

In the realm where thoughts meet despair,

Lonely hearts yearn for solace in the air.

For even in the dance of shadows' embrace,

Where secrets linger and memories ease the case.

And the deceiving sadness finds it's reprieve;

In souls who dare to feel and believe.

Invited are all the elves, the dwarfs, the fall,

The Witcher, the butcher and the wolves of Hati &
Skoll,
For this mystic realm is open for all;

So rise above them barriers and stand tall.

Know that everything ends and so will we,

For within our grasp lies the key;

To aid unlock the secrets of what could be.

A TALE OF YOUNG DESOLATION

In quiet corners of the school's embrace,

Where darkness looms and hopes have no place.

Silent wishes and the tales of dreams deferred.

Of youthful hearts that ache unheard.

Amidst the quandred halls and bustling thongs,

There lie lost souls singing silent songs;

One after 'other counting all their wrongs

Their laughter masked by the weight they bear,

Missing gratitude to homework they hear;

For their dreams are dimmed by the burdens they
share

In the dim glow of flickering light,

Where future seems distant, just out of sight;

At an early age, this responsibilty is akin fright.

And the weight of expectations crushes their glee,

For they struggle in silence forever longing to be free

Behind the forced smiles and weary eyes,

Lay tales of broken wings and muted cries.

For in the hallowed halls of academic delight,

Many hearts are heavy, far from light.

In this race for success and pressure to excel,

They navigate the labyrinth, each with a story to tell;

Of shattered hearts, the sacrifices,

And of the price they pay,

As the weight of the world grows day by day.

Yet in their quiet moments, they dare to dream,

To paint a future, way brighter than it may seem.

For within sadness that shadows their gaze,

Lies beauty and resilience ready to amaze.

PATH THROUGH GARDEN OF WEEDS

In the garden of weeds,

There's a path that leads,

To the starry sky; and to a lovely life's seed.

You the devil may take that path,

You a human may take that path,

Or you, the witcher may take that path,

And the same path could be taken by others.

On this oath tread the lonely,

The unwanted, and the happy.

For here there is no judge,

And the finale is life's judge.

Those who tread this path must know,

Undefeated they shall stand;

For this path is meant for bravery to show,

And not for one to just stand.

REFLECTIONS OF DESPAIR: COULD IT BE YOU OR ME?

Well aware of how much he's hated,

He hates himself, he's already stated;

Despite this he feels decapitated.

In these lonely crowded places,

The dark he embraces.

Can't distinguish 'tween ribbons and laces,

Fell from heaven, he lost his graces.

Like a bird he wishes to fly away,

And like a whale, drift.

Towards a world far away,

His reality displaced, he's lost in the rift.

No one wants him now,

And maybe no one ever will.

What will he do in a world, so seemingly still?

For he's our average guy;

yet with love and care nil.

In his roller coaster race against time.

In a place where he has,

Neither nickel nor a dime.

He looks for opportunities, a way to shine.

A place where, to blur the pain, he will smile.

May you forever read with glee,

Because he could be thee-

And he could be me.

<u>LOVE'S DUALITY, CURSE OR A BLESSING?</u>

When things take a violent turn,

Hearts are meant to burn.

Two hearts that once entwined,

Now in rejection, not intertwined .

When there's squander in love-

When the hearts accept,

And however so the mind may reject,

That is when heart becomes a suspect.

Those who once were friends,

Are now in denial, out of trends

They look, look and look yet again,

And again look for the love that's lost.

The fire place that was originally warm,

Has turned cold dur to thoughts that swarm.

And the love, which was once true,

Has turned 360 looking untrue.

Love could be a blessing as it could be a curse,

Accept it as 'tween good and evil a truce.

The betrayal love does is an evil curse,

While the care is a blessing good.

I, to you, in all likely hood,

Will prescribe to maintain,

Along love a tight brotherhood,

For sometimes it'll hurt;

Even when the care may retain

FIELD OF MEMORIES, A LOST BOND

In the garden of friendship, once in bloom,

A fragile rose withered too soon.

Its petals, vibrant, now dulled with despair,

A bond shattered, beyond repair.

In the depths of silence, where echoes wane,

A void echoes, filled with endless pain.

A cherished melody, now a haunting refrain,

A friendship severed, by anguish's chain.

Through the fields of memory, a gentle breeze,

Whispers of laughter, now stilled with unease.

A bond once sturdy, now fragile and frail,

Lost to shadows, where sorrow sets sail.

In the starlit expanse, where dreams take flight,

A soul departs, swallowed by the night.

A friend's absence, an ache that lingers,

In the heart's abyss, where grief's touch stings.

The echoes of laughter, now muffled cries,

In the wake of a friendship's demise.

A void that widens, a rift in the soul,

As memories cascade, beyond control.

In the garden of friendship, a rose now weeps,

For the bond that's broken, forever it keeps.

A friend lost to shadows' embrace,

Leaving behind a lingering trace.

<u>A SYMPHONY OF FLIGHT</u>

In skies of endless azure, where dreams take flight,

Birds adorn the canvas, a spectacular sight.

With wings outstretched, they dance in delight,

A joyful symphony, in the sun's warm light.

They soar with grace, on the wind's gentle breath,

Carving arcs of freedom, in life's vibrant breadth.

Their hearts like notes in a song, pure and sweet,

A serenade of joy, in every beat.

But among their songs of laughter and glee,

Lurk moments of sadness, like shadows at sea.

For the birds, like humans, bear hearts that weep,

In the deep of the night, when the world's asleep.

They, too, have felt the weight of sorrow's wing,

When storms descend and dark clouds sing.

Their tears, like rain, from the heavens they cry,

A reflection of human hearts, beneath the same sky.

In the fall of feathers, like tears shed in pain,

They share the depths of human heart's reign.

And when the night is cold, and hope is but a spark,

They show us the way to mend a heart, so dark

Their nests, like homes, are built with care,

Each twig a story, each leaf a prayer.

In their eyes, we see reflections of our own,

A world of emotion, in each heart, is sown.

In their joyful flight, we find our own delight,

In their tears, we glimpse our darkest night.

In the unity of sky and earth, we are bound,

A reminder that our hearts, in joy and sorrow, are found.

So, when you see birds soaring high,

Know they share our joys and tears in the sky.

Their hearts, like ours, a symphony that plays,

In the grand tapestry of life's ever-turning maze.

<u>HEART OF DECEIT</u>

In the shadows' embrace, a soul concealed,

An assassin's heart, a life revealed.

Forced by a world of cruelty and despair,

A life of shadows, no soul could repair.

Born from a cradle of cold deceit,

A puppet of darkness, in silent defeat.

Innocence stolen, a child no more,

Thrust into shadows, to settle a score.

The world, unforgiving, a master of lies,

Forced this path, beneath cruel skies.

A life of secrets, a cloak of disguise,

Where the truth is buried, the heart often cries.

In the silent night, where blades gleam bright,

They dance in shadows, out of sight.

A puppet of power, a puppet of might,

An assassin's world, cloaked in endless night.

Yet in the depths of their cold disguise,

Lurks a heart, hidden from prying eyes.

A glimmer of hope, a flicker of grace,

In a cruel world's unforgiving embrace.

For they, too, were once a heart untamed,

Before a cruel world left his soul maimed.

An assassin's fate, a life entwined,

With the world's cruelty, forever confined.

hopeful during the day, hopeless at night,

His work, art, to behold, a sorrowful sight.

For innocent souls he prays, effort forever pays,

The night will end and so will the days

In the silent hours, as the night unfolds,

A story untold, in whispers and codes.

An assassin's life, by the world imposed,

A tragic tale, in darkness enclosed.

<u>REVERIE OF DANCING LEAVES</u>

In the emerald glades, where whispers sigh,

A noble elf with a wistful eye.

Adorned in regalia, a crown of grace,

Longing for the world's simpler embrace.

Amidst the courtly dances and lofty affairs,

He yearns for a life stripped of pomp's ensnare.

A soul that craves the touch of the earth,

Beyond the trappings of nobility's birth.

In the tapestried halls, where shadows play,

He pines for the sun's unfiltered ray.

A spirit unbound, yet confined by duty,

Torn between honor and inner beauty.

With silken words, he masks his plight,

Draped in elegance, yet yearning for respite.

A heart that beats with a mortal's zest,

In a world where nobility deems the best.

But deep in the forest, where secrets dwell,

He sheds his façade, in a secluded spell.

Beneath the canopy's comforting shroud,

He seeks solace, away from the crowd.

There, he dances with the leaves and the breeze,

Embracing the world that his heart decrees.

In the quiet of nature, he finds his reprieve,

A noble elf, with a longing to believe.

For though his status binds him, in life's intricate weave,

His spirit soars, where the woods softly heave.

In the heart of the forest, he's just one of many,

A noble elf yearning to be free, yet burdened by his pedigree.

<u>A DREAM TO FORGE LEGENDS</u>

In a workshop nestled deep in stone,

A dwarf with dreams, so truly his own.

With hammer and fire, he toiled each day,

Crafting legends from twilight's gray.

His hands were strong, his heart was pure,

Determined to create a weapon, for sure.

A legendary blade, with magic's gleam,

A symbol of hope, a dreamer's dream

But the jeers and jests, his spirit wore,

From peers who mocked, and scorned him more.

"Such dreams are folly," they would say,

"Your legendary weapon will never see the light of day."

Yet the dwarf, undeterred, continued to strive,

With each swing of his hammer, he'd come alive.

His heart as resolute as the stones he'd hew,

To craft a legend, he knew he must pursue.

He forged through nights, he toiled through days,

His vision undimmed by the naysayers' dismays.

His weapon took shape, with a radiant gleam,

A legendary blade, the stuff of dream.

But when his peers saw the masterpiece done,

Their hearts were humbled, their ridicule undone.

For the dwarf had crafted, with love and with pride,

A weapon of legends, forever to bide.

In the end, the dwarf found his hope anew,

In the weapon he crafted, strong and true.

No longer brought down by his peers' disdain,

He'd turned their doubt into his gain.

A legendary weapon, his heart's greatest feat,

A testament to dreams that none can beat.

For in the face of despair and strife,

A dwarf's determination can forge a new life.

<u>TALES WHISPERED BY THE SEA</u>

In the ocean's wild embrace, they roam,

The unruly pirates, with hearts of foam.

Sails unfurled, to the winds they dance,

Plundering dreams with a ruthless glance.

Their laughter echoes through the salty air,

As they chart their course with little care.

On waves of rebellion, they stake their claim,

A lawless crew, chasing fortune's flame.

With a tint sadness, they opt to suffer alone,

fueled with regret, they hope to atone.

for sins committed, maybe in grief,

Lives on the line, they seek relief.

With cutlasses gleaming in the golden light,

They plunder and pillage through the night.

Mischief their muse, and chaos their guide,

They revel in the tempest, with nothing to hide.

Their tales whispered in taverns by the sea,

Of daring escapades, wild and free.

For they fear no law, no moral decree,

The unruly pirates, masters of the sea.

A facade of composure, swinging by the sea

Rum and booze, their ship, their glee.

Oh the tales sung, by bards on rum,

Showing their life, strings are strum.

But in the quiet hours, when storms subside,

And the moon's soft glow becomes their guide,

Regret whispers in the shadows deep,

As they ponder the secrets they forever keep.

For even the boldest hearts can yearn for peace,

Beyond the tumultuous tides that never cease.

In the hearts of unruly pirates, a longing lingers,

For a tranquil haven, where hope still lingers.

SYMPHONY OF A LONELY BARD

In shadows deep, where echoes weep,

There sits a bard, his soul to keep.

His notes, they rise, like lonesome sighs,

Yet weave a tale that softly tries.

Through tear-stained strings, his melodies glide,

Echoes of pain in the silence reside.

Each note a whisper, a delicate art,

He sings for joy, though bearing a heavy heart.

With every strum, his spirit unwinds,

In every lyric, solace he finds.

His forlorn voice, a gentle embrace,

A balm for hearts in the world's harsh space.

Though his own woes weigh heavy and long,

Foe them he crafts a symphony, a comfort song.

A lonely bard's tale, in the music's embrace,

Singing for joy, with sorrow's trace.

And he prays to sing for forever,

From sorrow he knows he'll never recover,

The bard's bloody path may never end;

For he prays,

The joyful songs may ese the sorrow within.

The tearful nights,

And his search for hopeful lights;

Despite everything,

For forever he'll smile, smile and smile.

FACADE OF COMPOSURE

In the labyrinth of his shattered dreams,

He wanders alone, where silence screams.

The weight he carries, a burden unseen,

A hidden tale in the shadows, it has been.

We see the surface, the mask he wears,

Neither the scars, the agony he bears,

Nor the fiery trials that forged his soul,

It's a journey through darkness, beyond control

Tearful rivers that silently flow,

Shaping the path where spirits grow.

We see the smiles, the facade he create,

Not the heartache, nor the battles of fate.

The battles he fought, unseen and unheard,

The demons he's faced, with every word.

You see the calm, the composed facade he'll portray,

Not the storms, nor the turmoil that won't sway.

Only the devil knows, the hell woven within,

The labyrinth of pain, where he's always been.

We know not the price, the sacrifices he's made,

In the shadows, the price of his soul paid.

Weeping in a foreign land, the land of dreams,

Where tears make the perfect streams;

Flowing from hidden mountains of despair,

Why must we say he's beyond repair?

<u>A JOURNEY UNMAPPED</u>

To reach a destination, without roadmap,

Leads to a tragic path akin a trap;

Where all may tremble, fall and die

Into a valley where light and hope feels like a lie.

The Phoenix sings a melancholy tale,

Then it vanishes away leaving ash so pale,

With life in darkness ever so stale.

And the crossroads this time present a choice,

Pick either Halloween, Christmas, then you better rejoice.

For the unending path, will come to an end,

And the straight lines can forever bend.

So lift the safety valve,

Breathe in the fresh air of forests amidst.

The trees, the leaves & the soil alike,

Both ways on a mountain one shall hike.

The world cares naught for what you think,

Like a ghost then, live life on the brink.

Always be ready to fall and disappear,

For only then will your angles appear.

<u>IN MEMORY OF SCARIFICE</u>

The Witcher may wish upon death,

And he'd be be thrilled when it looms.

For the Witcher has suppressed all gloom;

As he stands in silence wishing upon death.

Regrets? He has many,

For he lives in the valley of plenty;

Killing away and upon his sorrows

For ever wishing upon peaceful tomorrows.

His wolf dear, howls for him

And his raven forever sings to him;

For they're his only companions in this life so still,

That now is crumbling upon the twilight hill.

People said they'll comeback, they never do,

For in his weeded path he has learned to judge too.

Defiant as rebels they tend to meet him,

And go back home wrapped in flags and smiles dim.

The Witcher wears his badge,

Despite the dangers.

He defends his people,

Yet seldom go down in literatures.

His fellows, he's seen meeting death,

He recalls, with a smile away they went.

For them patriots we have the army,

For those who for their nation will die.

May we never forget their sacrifice,

For the Witcher will do it

Be it once twice or thrice.

A FESTIVAL OF LIGHTS

In the tapestry of night, a celestial dance,

Where stars alight, in a cosmic trance.

Amid the velvet dark, a whisper ignites,

A tale of wonder, of profound delights.

From the embers of dusk, a festival awakes,

In the heart of the shadows, where magic takes.

A symphony of hues, a symphony of sights,

A celebration of hope, in the darkest nights.

The city adorns its soul in radiant attire,

With lanterns that shimmer, like souls on fire.

A kaleidoscope of dreams, in every hue,

As the festival of lights, is brought anew.

The streets pulsate with a vibrant zeal,

As hearts resonate with the festive appeal.

A mosaic of joy, painted in gold and red,

A tribute to life, where worries are shed.

Each flicker of flame, a prayer

in disguise,

A beacon of faith that forever implies,

The triumph of good over darkness's art,

In the festival of lights, that kindles the heart.

As the night cascades with a shimmering grace,

And shadows recede, leaving no trace.

The festival of lights, a tale of hope,

A reminder that in darkness, we can cope.

So, let us bask in the glow of its embrace,

And find solace in its warm, gentle grace.

For in the festival of lights, we find our way,

Through the darkest of nights, into the day.

AN ETERNAL BATTLE GROUND OF COSMIC CONFLICTS

In realms unseen, where shadows dance,

A cosmic battle, fates' wild chance.

Heaven's guardians and Hell's fierce horde,

Clash in the cosmos, their conflict poured.

Demons of fire, with eyes ablaze,

Angels with wings, in a celestial haze.

Battleground eternal, where realms entwine,

A war untold, of the divine.

In the cosmic theater, emotions ignite,

Anguish and love, in the eternal fight.

Demons wield envy, a venomous sting,

Angels with grace, hope's gentle wing.

The echoes of wrath, in Hell's fiery sea,

Clash with the serenity of Heaven's decree.

A symphony of conflict, emotions untamed,

In the cosmic dance, where destinies are named.

Fear, a demon's whisper, in shadows profound,

Hope, an angelic chorus, a celestial sound.

Pride, a fiery tempest, in Hell's inferno,

Compassion, a beacon, in Heaven's eternal glow.

Jealousy's flames lick the edges of strife,

Harmony's melody, the rhythm of life.

Lust's seduction, in the infernal abyss,

Devotion's embrace, in celestial bliss.

A dance of dichotomy, the yin and the yang,

In the cosmic tapestry, where emotions hang.

As the battle unfolds, in the realms above,

Human hearts mirror, this eternal love.

For within the mortal coil, the battleground here,

Demons and angels, within us appear.

Envy, pride, and wrath, in shadows reside,

Yet hope, love, and compassion, by our side.

The cosmic conflict, a mirror held true,

In the human heart, the battleground grew.

Heaven and hell, within us entwined,

A tapestry of emotions, in the fabric of the mind.

In the grand celestial theater, emotions declare,

The eternal struggle, the cosmic affair.

Yet amidst the chaos, a truth to unveil,

In the heart's battleground, humanity sails.

<u>WHEN WORLDS UNFOLD</u>

In the quiet alcove of a sunlit room,

A book lover sits, lost in the gloom.

Pages whisper tales, as worlds unfold,

Imagination's treasures, stories untold.

The dusty volumes, like portals unseen,

Transport the reader, where dreams convene.

A gentle breeze through the parchment sighs,

Inviting the soul to fantastical skies.

In the hallowed space where reality bends,

A magic carpet of words ascends.

From the worn spines, enchantment takes flight,

As characters dance in the soft twilight.

Among the shelves of endless lore,

A rustle of pages, a creaking door.

From the ink-stained realms, they start to emerge,

Fantasy characters, ready to surge.

A dragon, fierce with scales of flame,

A wizard, master of the arcane.

Elves with eyes that shimmer like stars,

And knights, who've braved countless wars.

A heroine, bold with a heart so true,

And a villain, with shadows that grew.

They step from the pages, alive in the air,

A tapestry woven with dreams to share.

The book lover, wide-eyed and amazed,

In this literary haven, a world is raised.

Through whispered verses and epic prose,

A fantastical symphony, emotions compose.

The dragon breathes fire, a warmth so divine,

The wizard conjures, a spell in rhyme.

The elves dance gracefully in the moonlit night,

And the knights stand proud, in armor bright.

Yet in this encounter, emotions entwine,

As the characters speak, a connection they find.

The book lover's heart, a rhythm unmet,

A melody played, an emotional duet.

The dragon's eyes, kindred to the fire,

The wizard's wisdom, a yearning desire.

Elves' laughter, like a gentle stream,

Knights' bravery, in a moonbeam gleam.

Through the pages, a bond does grow,

As the characters and reader, together bestow.

A journey of words, emotions unfurl,

In the magical embrace of a book lover's world.

As the final chapters draw near,

The characters retreat, whispers in the ear.

Yet, in the heart's library, their echoes reside,

A timeless connection, in pages confide.

SANDS OF OLD:
ECHOES OF LOST POETS

In whispers of time, where echoes fade,

Linger the tales of poets, in silence laid.

Their verses once danced, with passionate grace,

Now lost in the shadows, no echo to trace.

Through parchment and ink, their spirits roamed,

Weaving emotions, where hearts once comb.

Yet their words, like petals, wither and decay,

Lost in the currents of life's relentless sway.

In the annals of history, their echoes reside,

Whispers of sonnets, where passions abide.

Their tales, like murmurs in the evening breeze,

Echoes of longing, in forgotten pleas.

In the chambers of memory, their voices wane,

Fading whispers of love, of joy, and of pain.

Lost in the ether, their stories unfold,

Tales of lost poets, in the sands of old.

Their ink now dries, their quills at rest,

In the tapestry of time, their legacy blessed.

Their verses still linger, though poets are gone,

Their tales, a reminder of life's bittersweet song.

A LOST CHILDHOOD, UNSEEN WOUNDS

In shadows cast by youthful dreams,

A teen awakens, choked by screams,

Of a past too heavy to comprehend,

A childhood lost, a world to mend.

"I've spent my days in mending wounds,

That scarred my soul too soon, too soon,"

Too young to grasp life's bitter sting,

Too early to wear this suffering.

Ghosts of grief now haunt my days,

Where laughter once held vibrant sway,

Children should dance, happy and free,

Not bear the weight of what shouldn't be.

"Don't preach of strength from trials borne,

I know this path, I've walked, I've worn.

I could have been a child, carefree,

Instead, forced to grow, forced to be."

The guardians, their pledge betrayed,

Left him alone, lost in this charade,

No healing balm can staunch this ache,

No solace found in the words they make.

"Damn right, my anger finds its place,

I'll never reclaim that stolen space,

Of innocent days, laughter in play,

My childhood lost, too soon, away."

In the ashes of what could have been,

A teen stands, wounded, yet unseen,

An anger brewing, a sorrow deep,

For a childhood lost, forever to keep.

TWILIT LEGACY OF THE VANISHING BIRTHRIGHT

In shadows cast by a somber moon's glow,

A child once held a kingdom's untold woe.

Beneath the canopy of starry plight,

Lies a tale of loss, veiled in the night.

His father, regal in valor and might,

Fell to a fate in the silence of night.

A throne unclaimed, a kingdom in tears,

Left a void in hearts, entwined with fears.

His mother, burdened with grief's cruel weight,

Sold her son to a fate separate.

To shield him from a cruel game,

She traded his innocence, name, and claim.

Unaware, the child wandered alone,

Not yet a crown to bear, or kingdom to own.

In tender years, devoid of his past,

He trudged through life's tempestuous blast.

No regal halls echoed with his voice,

No tender touch, no maternal choice.

Sold for protection, a secret so deep,

Left to wander, to suffer, to weep.

He dreamed of thrones an admiring grace,

Unseen, unheard, in a forgotten place.

A knight in guise, a pauper's disguise,

Lost in a world, where hope slowly dies.

Forlorn, he roamed, a lone orphaned heir,

Unraveling tales, unaware and unaware.

A shattered legacy, a fragmented truth,

His lineage lost to his youth.

So the child grew in the shadows' embrace,

Never fathomed his lineage or royal trace.

Sold for survival, from crown to clay,

A tragic pawn in a kingdom's dismay.

Yet in the depth of his dimming soul's sight,

Lies the specter of a vanished birthright.

A child robbed of what was never known,

Destined to wander, forever alone.

Yet that child suffered and fought,

For even a day, he did not stop.

In the never reckoning valley of desire,

He dreamed to be the king and light it on fire

<u>LIES: A DUAL EDGED BLADE</u>

In the shadows' grip, where darkness reigns,

Lies emerge, like silent chains.

A dual-edged blade, with edges keen,

Carving wounds on truths unseen.

Whispers slither through the night,

Cloaked in deceit, a chilling fright.

A dance of shadows, a macabre waltz,

As lies entwine, ensnare, and false truths exalt.

On one side, the deceiver grins,

Crafting tales where falsehood begins.

Yet on the other, a wounded soul,

Bleeding trust, a fractured whole.

The blade of lies, a sinister dance,

A haunting melody, a spectral trance.

It cuts through bonds with stealthy might,

Leaving scars on both sides of the night.

Faces masked, intentions veiled,

A symphony of deceit, the truth assailed.

In the eerie silence of the deceitful dance,

Echoes the pain, the lies enhance.

A ghostly specter of trust betrayed,

Lingers in the fog where shadows played.

The dual-edged blade, relentless and cold,

Leaves a tale of sorrow, both young and old.

So beware the dance of the lying blade,

Its haunting notes, a dirge replayed.

For in the end, when the music subsides,

It leaves behind desolation on both divides.

A FARMER'S DESPRATE END

In the fields of dust and sorrow, I stood,

Parched and weary, like the trees of wood.

A mirror to nature, my reflection dry,

A symphony of despair, beneath the unforgiving sky.

The wind whispered tales of a life misspent,

Tattered curtains danced, my remorseful lament.

Endless questions echoed, haunting my soul,

What have I done? What was my role?

The answers emerged, stark on paper white,

A revelation bold, in shadows of the night.

I am done, a prisoner of my fate,

Helpless farmer, burdened by weight.

Hopeless husband, in the darkness lost,

A useless father, at a great, painful cost.

Possessed by a spirit, I rose from despair,

Tripped, slipped, and fell, as if life weren't fair.

At last, I arrived at destiny's gate,

A well of reflection, sealing my fate.

Watery eyes met a reflection so bleak,

"I'm sorry," I whispered, my voice so meek.

In the depths, a plunge, a final farewell,

A somber journey to the watery well.

Congratulations, society, witness my strife,

In death's embrace, I surrender my life.

<u>A STORY UNTOLD</u>

In shadows cast by fleeting light,

Untold stories hide from sight.

Whispers linger, tales unsaid,

Lost within the pages unread.

Silent narratives, unheard cries,

In hidden realms where mystery lies.

Echoes of the untold song,

Longing to be shared, belong.

But who will listen to their plea,

In the depths of night's mystery?

For every heart holds secrets deep,

In the shadows, they silently keep.

The moon may rise, the stars may shine,

Yet the secrets remain, a sacred sign.

Of lives lived in silent reverie,

Yearning for ears willing to see.

So let us be the ones to hear,

The whispers of stories, crystal clear.

To bring light to the hidden night,

And let untold tales take flight.

For in the shadows, beauty lies,

In the untold, the unspoken cries.

Let us be the ones to lend an ear,

To the stories that long to appear.

<u>CACOPHONY OF SERENDIPTY</u>

In the fields of shadows and despair, I stood,

Bound by the threads of fate, misunderstood.

A prisoner of science, a pawn in the game,

A spectrum of motives, no two the same.

The room, a crucible of time and trial,

A canvas for anguish, a vessel in denial.

The silence, a companion, cold and vast,

A symphony of questions, in echoes cast.

Days of monotony, a relentless routine,

Hyperborean soup, stale bread, a mundane cuisine.

Exercises to hone a body, a weapon of might,

Yet the missing memories, an endless night.

A man with a rictus smile, a messenger of change,

Whispers of a world, beyond the range.

Corridors twisted, etched with hues bizarre,

A door, a revelation, a portal ajar.

A circular table, a map of the world,

A revelation, a banner unfurled.

Lilith, a leader with hazel eyes gleaming,

A tale unfolds, a world redeeming.

The roots of a disease, the Craze takes hold,

A world enslaved, its stories untold.

SAPIEN, a group fighting the machine,

A plea for help, a chance to intervene.

A genetic anomaly, immune to the plague,

A value assigned, a role to engage.

Emrys, Morgan, Daryn, kin and allies,

A unit forged, under starlit skies.

Training days, nights of shared tales,

A bond forming, as emotion prevails.

A journey from existence to living,

A transformation, in the act of forgiving.

A mission arises, a threat to face,

A woman with drugs, a dangerous embrace.

Betrayals and battles, a dance of fate,

A revelation, at Twelfth Bridge's gate.

Lilith's deceit, a sinister design,

A serum injected, a moment malign.

Dreams of fire, a world consumed,

A destiny rewritten, a life exhumed.

Awakening to pain, to a world unknown,

A struggle for survival, in shadows thrown.

An unexpected mercy, a test to endure,

A realization, of motives impure.

In the end, a choice to make,

To pull the trigger, or the truth to forsake.

The shades of grey, the complexities unfold,

A journey through chaos, a story retold.

A28

<u>WHISPERS OF AN UNFULFILLED APOCALYPSE</u>

In the twilight of despair, the world met its supposed demise,

A tale of innocence lost, veiled in sorrow's guise.

The End of the World, a chilling prophecy foretold,

Yet amidst the chaos, a poignant story unfolds.

Two friends, Ariyan and I, young and unaware,

Caught in the web of fate, a burden we could not bear.

Media's whispers, doom's impending call,

A surreal narrative that left our hearts enthralled.

Ariyan, not gripped by fear, but an unusual glee,

His secret harbored, a revelation yet to be.

Cycling through muddy lanes, with a smile so wide,

A week later, his truth in shadows would hide.

28th October 2016, the day of reckoning, approached fast,

Yet life went on, oblivious to the impending blast.

A world unfazed, walking dogs, sharing coffee sips,

Unaware that existence hung by fragile clips.

Ariyan, my confidant, a mystery untold,

His revelation awaited, emotions yet to unfold.

He appeared, cycling with that familiar grin,

An explanation overdue, a tale of loss and sin.

His sister, Arisha, in the throes of fate,

Her time slipping away, an inevitable wait.

Ariyan, calm and composed, a strange serenity,

A conviction that death was a twisted blessing's decree.

Arisha's smile, her hands on his cheek so cold,

A moment frozen in time, a story to be retold.

Revelations of an impending end, a cosmic closure,

The world, a stage, for an eternal composure.

A seamless transition to an "Unknown" embrace,

A belief that death was a unifying grace.

The clock struck midnight, the appointed hour near,

Yet, the apocalypse was not what we had come to fear.

Silence prevailed, no cataclysmic show,

A world unchanged, as the night let go.

Days later, Ariyan's smile vanished without a trace,

His innocence shattered, a mask replaced.

In the wake of unfulfilled prophecies, tears cascade,

A tale of an apocalypse, a friendship betrayed.

Arisha, in eternal slumber, the green line flat,

A poignant reminder of innocence gone, a tragic spat.

Ariyan, a ghost in the city of dreams,

Moved away, lost is home's chaotic streams.

On the first dawn of Halloween, reality did bend,

For me alone, on that day, the world did end.

TALE OF ATLAF'S SIXTH SENSE

In the quiet corridors of unseen realms,

Where senses linger, beyond what overwhelms.

A tale unfolds of a sixth sense profound,

In mysteries of fate, where answers are found.

Not by choice, but an ethereal grace,

A clairvoyant journey, a peculiar embrace.

In the tapestry of life, a thread unseen,

A guide named Altaf, in realms between.

The skeptic heart, once veiled in doubt,

Encountered a man whose whispers devout.

Through phones, not eyes, the visions unfurled,

A dance of voices in another world.

Altaf, a sage in humble abode,

With powers unseen, a mystical code.

His cot, a haven of ropes and straw,

A telephone, his cosmic flaw.

No riches adorned his modest space,

Yet gratitude poured, a heartfelt trace.

For voices reaching from afar,

Seeking solace beneath life's enigmatic star.

A friend in need, burdened by strife,

Sought answers in the tapestry of life.

Altaf listened, no questions, no probe,

Predicting changes, an overseas globe.

A tale unfolded, a prophecy true,

In the heart of Kampala, dreams anew.

A skeptic's doubt turned awe-struck gaze,

As life mirrored Altaf's enigmatic maze.

Yet Altaf, the seer, confessed no might,

No conscious powers in the guiding light.

Forces unseen, a cosmic thread,

In his own mystery, he quietly tread.

An unsung hero, in realms unknown,

Altaf, a savior, compassionately shown.

A selfless saint, a guiding star,

Whispers of grace from distances far.

In the realm of doubt, a story told,

Of Altaf's wisdom, a narrative bold.

Through vibrations in the voice, a cosmic art,

A tapestry woven, a compassionate heart.

"In the symphony of lost echoes, the most profound melodies are composed by those who learn to dance in the rhythm of their own uncertainties."

9 798889 277171 9